A WORLD OF RECIPES

China

REVISED AND UPDATED

Julie McCulloch

Heinemann
LIBRARY

www.heinemannlibrary.co.uk
Visit our website to find out more information about Heinemann Library books.

To order:
☎ Phone +44 (0) 1865 888066
🖹 Fax +44 (0) 1865 314091
🖳 Visit www.heinemannlibrary.co.uk

Edited by David Andrews and Diyan Leake
Designed by Richard Parker
Illustrated by Nicholas Beresford-Davis
Picture research by Mica Brancic
Originated by Chroma Graphics (Overseas) Pte Ltd
Printed and bound in China by Leo Paper Products Ltd

ISBN 978 0 431 11816 1 (hardback)
13 12 11 10 09
10 9 8 7 6 5 4 3 2 1

ISBN 978 0 431 11828 4 (paperback)
13 12 11 10 09
10 9 8 7 6 5 4 3 2 1

British Library Cataloguing in Publication Data
McCulloch, Julie, 1973-
  China. - 2nd ed. - (A world of recipes)
A full catalogue record for this book is available from the British Library.

Acknowledgments
We would like to thank the following for permission to reproduce photographs: © Capstone Global Library Ltd/ MM Studios pp. **14**, **15**; Gareth Boden pp. **8–13**, **16–43**; Photolibrary Group pp. **5** (Mauritius/Rafael Macia), **6** (Reso/ Charbonneau Charbonneau), **7** (Creatas).

Cover photograph of fried shrimps with vegetables and a bowl of rice reproduced with permission of Getty Images (StockFood Creative/Klaus Arras).

Every effort has been made to contact copyright holders of material reproduced in this book. Any omissions will be rectified in subsequent printings if notice is given to the publisher.

All the Internet addresses (URLs) given in this book were valid at the time of going to press. However, due to the dynamic nature of the Internet, some addresses may have changed, or sites may have changed or ceased to exist since publication. While the author and publisher regret any inconvenience this may cause readers, no responsibility for any such changes can be accepted by either the author or the publisher.

Contents

Key: *easy **medium ***difficult

China 4

Chinese food 6

Ingredients 8

Before you start 10

Mushroom and water chestnut soup .... 12 **

Steamed tofu with egg .... 14 *

Prawns with ginger sauce .... 16 *

Chinese fish cakes .... 18 **

Stir-fried fish with mushrooms and cucumber .... 20 **

Lemon chicken stir-fry .... 22 **

Honey chicken .... 24 **

Noodles with minced pork .... 26 **

Vegetable chow mein .... 28 **

Tofu stir-fry .... 30 **

Celery and prawn salad .... 32 *

Ginger and spring onion noodles .... 34 **

Three rice dishes .... 36 *

Sweet chestnut balls .... 38 *

Chocolate lychees .... 40 **

Orange tea .... 42 *

Further information 44

Healthy eating 45

Glossary 46

Index 48

Some words are shown in bold, **like this**. You can find out what they mean by looking in the glossary.

China

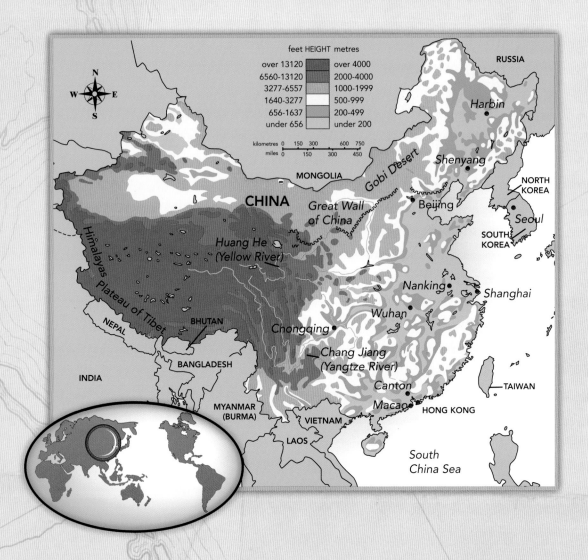

More people live in the People's Republic of China than in any other country. This great nation rose up from a land that is as varied as its people.

China is in eastern Asia, beside the Pacific Ocean. To the southwest stand the Himalayas, the world's highest mountains. The Gobi Desert lies in the middle of China. In the east, flatter land is used for farming.

The mountains have a cold climate with snow all year. Northern China is also cold. Rainforests grow in the south. In winter, monsoon winds blow from the north, causing cold, dry weather. In summer, monsoons blow in from the ocean. This causes warm weather with heavy rain.

In the past

China is a civilization with thousands of years of written history. The Chinese invented paper. Books were written using calligraphy, an artistic style of ink writing. Later, printing methods were invented. Many ancient records exist about Chinese life.

For centuries, emperors ruled China. They lived in a palace called the Forbidden City, which was built of marble and **tropical** wood. It had over a thousand buildings inside moats and walls. Emperors also had stone walls built along the country's northern border. They wanted to keep out tribes including the Mongols. Parts of this defence system, called the Great Wall, still stand.

China traded with the west (Europe) along a route called the Silk Road. The Buddhist religion entered from India along this route. Silk, cotton, and porcelain were important Chinese trade goods. For many years, only the Chinese knew the secret of how to spin silk threads from the cocoon of the silk worm. This made silk fabric very costly.

↑ Statues of lions stand in front of the Forbidden City.

Special times in China

Chinese people continue to honour traditions. They use their own calendar. Their zodiac has twelve years represented by animals. Maybe you were born in the year of the snake, or the tiger! At New Year, everyone celebrates their birthday, no matter when they were born. Firecrackers are lit and lion dancers perform in the streets.

Chinese food

The growth of Chinese civilization depended upon two grains: millet and rice. About 7,000 years ago, millet was grown in the north, by the Yellow River. Villages were built where millet could be grown. Rice was first planted in the wetter climate of the south. As more rice was grown, more people could live in China. Today different kinds of rice are planted in both southern and northern China.

Around the country

Cooking varies between regions because of differences in climate and local traditions. There are eight kinds of Chinese cooking. They are called the Eight Great Traditions. A common saying about Chinese cooking is "East is sweet, South is salty, West is sour, North is spicy."

↑ These people are planting rice in the Chinese province of Yunnan.

Chinese meals

Chinese food is usually prepared in bite-size pieces and eaten using chopsticks. Each person is given a bowl of rice. The other food is placed in the middle of the table for everyone to share. Usually, rice is eaten every day. It might be served at breakfast as a porridge. For lunch and supper, it is often steamed. In a traditional greeting, people ask, "Have you had your rice today?"

Red meat is eaten less often than fish or chicken. **Vegetarian** dishes include mushrooms, bean sprouts, and leafy vegetables such as pak choi. **Stir-frying**, a method of **frying** vegetables in a pan, has been common since the Tang Dynasty (618–907 AD). Tofu is sometimes served in a stir-fry instead of meat. It is made from soy beans and is high in **protein**.

Festival foods

Red is the colour of happiness in China. Red foods are served at weddings and at the New Year. Other foods with special meanings are also served at the New Year. A whole chicken means family togetherness. Noodles mean long life, so it's bad luck to cut them. Fish served with the head and tail left on means a good beginning and good ending to the year.

↑ Mooncakes like these are eaten to celebrate the harvest festival in China.

Ingredients

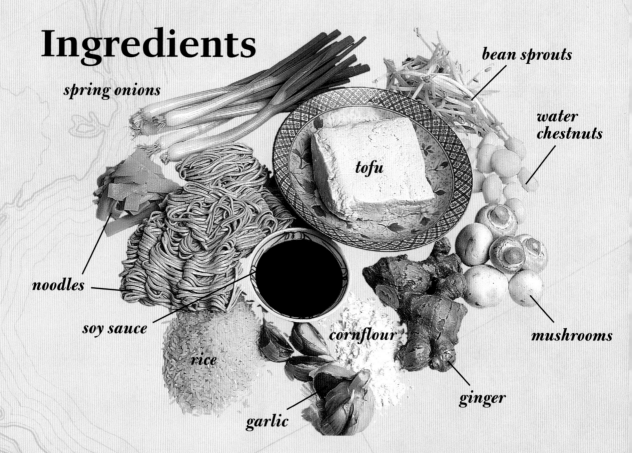

spring onions

bean sprouts

water chestnuts

tofu

noodles

soy sauce

rice

garlic

cornflour

ginger

mushrooms

Chinese cooking uses quite simple ingredients – fresh vegetables, fish, or meat, with a small amount of sauce to bring out their flavour.

Cornflour

Cornflour is used in China to thicken sauces. It is often used as part of a sauce called a marinade, as it helps the sauce coat the food. Cornflour is easy to buy.

Garlic

Garlic is used in many Chinese dishes. You can find garlic in the vegetable section of most food shops or supermarkets.

Ginger

Fresh ginger is used in many Chinese dishes, usually **peeled** and **grated**, or finely **chopped**. Ginger is readily available in supermarkets. It is much better to use fresh rather than dried ginger, as its flavour is stronger.

Noodles

There are many different types of noodles in China. Some are made from wheat and egg, some from rice, and some from ground-up beans. The recipes in this book suggest using dried wheat and egg noodles. You should find these noodles, usually just called "egg noodles", in packets in most supermarkets.

Oil

Chinese food is often cooked in sesame oil, made from sesame seeds. If you cannot find any, use vegetable oil instead for these recipes.

Rice

Rice is served with many Chinese dishes. It comes in two main types – short grain and long grain. Chinese people use long grain rice for most of their dishes.

Soy sauce

Soy sauce is made from soya beans, flour, salt, and water. It is very salty, so you don't need to add any extra salt to your food if it contains soy sauce. You can find soy sauce in most supermarkets.

Tofu

Tofu is made from pulped soya beans. It is called *doufu* in Chinese, but tofu in most countries. You can find tofu in most supermarkets.

Vegetables

Chinese cooking uses lots of fresh vegetables, some of which are more familiar outside China than others. The main vegetables used in the recipes in this book are bamboo shoots, bean sprouts, mushrooms, spring onions, and water chestnuts. It is easy to buy fresh mushrooms, spring onions, and bean sprouts but you may need to buy canned bamboo shoots and water chestnuts.

Before you start

Which recipe should I try?

The recipes you choose to make depends on many things. Some recipes make a good main course, while others are better as starters. Some are easy, others are more difficult.

The top right-hand page of each recipe has information that can help you. It tells you how long each recipe will take and how many people it serves. You can multiply or divide the quantities if you want to cook for more or fewer people. This section also shows how difficult each dish is to make: the recipes are easy (*), medium (**), or difficult (***) to cook. The symbols in the corner can help you quickly find certain recipes. Here is a key that will help you.

 Healthy choice: These recipes are healthy to eat.

 Quick and easy: These recipes are quick and easy to make.

 Sweet treat: These recipes make a good dessert or sweet snack.

This symbol ⚠ is sign of a dangerous step in a recipe. For these steps, take extra care or ask an adult to help.

Kitchen rules

There are a few basic rules you should always follow when you cook:

- Ask an adult if you can use the kitchen.
- Wash your hands before you start.
- Wear an apron to protect your clothes. Tie back long hair.
- Be very careful when using sharp knives.
- Never leave pan handles sticking out – it could be dangerous if you bump into them.
- Always wear oven gloves to lift things in and out of the oven.
- Wash fruit and vegetables before you use them.

Quantities and measurements

Ingredients for recipes can be measured in two different ways. Metric measurements use grams, litres, and millilitres. Imperial measurements use cups, ounces, and fluid ounces. In the recipes in this book you will see the following abbreviations:

tbsp = tablespoons   oz = ounces
tsp = teaspoons   ml = millilitres
g = grams   cm = centimetres

Utensils

To cook the recipes in this book, you will need these utensils, as well as kitchen essentials, such as forks, spoons, plates, and bowls.

- chopping board
- **colander**
- double boiler
- food processor or blender
- frying pan
- grater
- heatproof bowl
- large, flat, ovenproof dish
- measuring jug
- saucepan with lid
- set of scales
- sharp knife
- steamer
- whisk
- **wok** (if you don't have a wok, you can use a large frying pan instead)
- wooden spoon

Mushroom and water chestnut soup

In China, soup is often served between courses. You could also eat this light soup as a starter or for lunch.

What you need

1 onion
100g mushrooms
50g canned water chestnuts
50g canned bamboo shoots
2 spring onions
500ml water
1 vegetable stock cube
1 tbsp soy sauce

What you do

1 **Peel** the onion and finely **chop** it.

2 **Slice** the mushrooms.

3 **Drain** the liquid from the canned water chestnuts and bamboo shoots.

4 Cut the tops and bottoms off the spring onions, and finely chop them.

5 Put the water into a saucepan, and bring it to the **boil**. Crumble the stock cube into the water, and stir until it **dissolves**. Reduce the heat to a **simmer**.

6 Add the chopped onion and soy sauce to the stock. Simmer it for 10 minutes.

7 Add the mushrooms, water chestnuts, and bamboo shoots. Simmer the soup for a further 5 minutes.

8 Carefully take the soup off the heat. Stir in the chopped spring onions.

MUSHROOMS

Over 300 different kinds of mushroom are grown in China! You could try experimenting with different types of mushroom in this dish. Oyster mushrooms and shiitake mushrooms are some of the Chinese mushrooms you might be able to find in your local greengrocer's shop or supermarket.

shiitake mushrooms

oyster mushrooms

Steamed tofu with egg

Tofu originated in ancient China. It is made by separating soya milk into curds which are then pressed into blocks. Tofu has very little flavour or smell on its own, so it can be used either in savoury or sweet dishes, and is often seasoned or **marinated** to suit the dish. It is very nutritious and is a good source of **protein**, iron, and calcium.

What you need

2 eggs
½ tbsp soy sauce
1 tsp sesame oil
1 tsp cornflour
½ tsp salt
¼ tsp pepper
300g tofu
1 spring onion

What you do

1 **Beat** the eggs in a medium-sized bowl.

2 Add the soy sauce, oil, cornflour, salt, and pepper to the egg and beat all these ingredients together. Use a spoon to work any cornflour lumps against the side of the bowl to make a smooth mixture.

3 Roughly **chop** the tofu into chunks.

4 Add the tofu to the egg mixture and combine well.

5 Spoon the mixture into heat-proof serving dishes.

6 Place the dishes inside a steamer and steam for 10 minutes.

7 While the tofu is steaming, chop the spring onion into small pieces.

8 Scatter the spring onion pieces over the steamed tofu and serve.

Prawns with ginger sauce

This dish combines lots of typical Chinese flavours – seafood, ginger, soy sauce, and vinegar. You need to allow 30 minutes for the prawns to **marinate** in the sauce before you cook them. If possible, use large prawns, such as tiger prawns. You can use frozen prawns, but **defrost** them completely by moving them from the freezer to the fridge at least 12 hours before using them.

What you need

A small piece of fresh ginger (about 2cm long)

1 tbsp soy sauce

1 tbsp vegetable oil

1 tbsp wine vinegar (red or white)

225g cooked peeled prawns

A few sprigs of fresh parsley

What you do

1 **Peel** the skin from the ginger, and **grate** or finely **chop** it.

2 Mix together the soy sauce, oil, wine vinegar, and chopped ginger in an ovenproof dish.

3 Add the prawns, and stir them into the mixture so that they are well coated.

4 Leave the prawns to marinate for 30 minutes.

5 While the prawns are marinating, chop the parsley.

6 When the prawns have marinated, turn the grill on to a medium setting. Put the dish of marinated prawns under the grill.

7 **Grill** the prawns for 5 minutes, stirring them occasionally.

8 Put the grilled prawns onto plates, and sprinkle the parsley over them.

Chinese Fish Cakes

Fish cakes (or fish balls, as they are sometimes called) are very popular in China. Some can be **fried**, as shown here, others are **boiled** in water or stock. You could serve them with rice (see page 19) or noodles (see page 26). If you are using frozen fish fillets, make sure you **defrost** them completely by moving them from the freezer to the fridge at least 12 hours before you want to use them.

What You need

2 fish fillets
2 spring onions
1 clove garlic
1 tsp sugar
1 tsp soy sauce
2 tbsp vegetable oil
2 tbsp cornflour

What You do

1 Put the fish fillets into a food processor or blender. **Blend** them on a medium setting until they are in tiny pieces.

2 Cut the tops and bottoms off the spring onions, and finely **chop** them.

3 **Peel** the skin from the garlic clove, and finely chop it.

4 Put the fish, spring onions, and garlic into a bowl. Add the sugar, soy sauce, and half the oil.

5 Using your fingers, mix everything together. Add about half the cornflour to bind the mixture together.

6 Sprinkle the rest of the cornflour onto a chopping board or work surface. Tip the fish cake mixture onto it and divide it into four pieces.

7 Gently shape each piece into a circle, coating the outside in cornflour.

8 Heat the rest of the oil in a non-stick frying pan over a medium heat. Add the fish cakes, and fry them for about 10 minutes, turning them occasionally to cook both sides.

9 Serve the fish cakes hot or cold.

PLAIN BOILED RICE

Many Chinese dishes are served with rice. This recipe makes enough plain boiled rice for 2 people (see also page 36).

1 Put 140g rice into a saucepan.
2 Add 400ml water.
3 Bring to the boil, then simmer for 20 minutes, stirring occasionally, until the rice has soaked up all the water.

Stir-fried fish with mushrooms and cucumber

You could use fish such as Pacific cod, tilapia, or red snapper in this recipe. If you're using frozen fish fillets, **defrost** them by moving them from the freezer to the fridge at least 12 hours before using them. Serve with plain boiled rice (see page 19).

What you need

2 fish fillets
1 tbsp soy sauce
2 tsp cornflour
1 small cucumber
40g mushrooms
1 clove of garlic
A small piece of fresh
    ginger (about
    2cm long)
150ml water
2 tbsp vegetable oil
1 vegetable stock
    cube

What you do

1 Cut the fish fillets into pieces.

2 Mix together the soy sauce and the cornflour in a bowl. Add the fish pieces, and leave them to **marinate** for about an hour.

3 While the fish is marinating, thinly **slice** the cucumber and mushrooms.

4 **Peel** the garlic and finely **chop** it.

5 Peel the ginger, and **grate** or finely chop it.

6 Put 150ml water into a saucepan, and bring it to the **boil**. Crumble the stock cube into the water, and stir until it **dissolves**. Put the stock to one side.

7 When the fish has marinated, heat the oil in a **wok** or frying pan over a medium heat. Carefully put the fish pieces and the marinade into the wok.

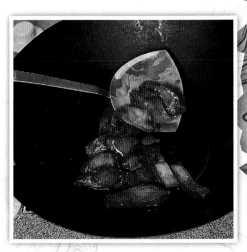

8 Add the sliced mushrooms, cucumber pieces, garlic, and ginger to the wok. **Stir-fry** for 2 minutes.

9 Add the vegetable stock. Reduce the heat, cook for 10 minutes, then serve.

21

Lemon chicken stir-fry

To make this dish, the chicken needs to be left to **marinate** in the lemon juice and soy sauce, so that it absorbs all their flavours. Try serving it with plain boiled rice (see page 19).

What you need

2 boneless chicken breasts

4 tbsp lemon juice

1 tbsp soy sauce

2 tsp cornflour

1 clove of garlic

1 tbsp vegetable oil

50g canned water chestnuts

25g canned bamboo shoots

What you do

1 Take any skin off the chicken breasts and **slice** them.

2 Mix together the soy sauce, the cornflour, and 2 tbsp of the lemon juice in a bowl. Add the chicken, turning it several times so that it is well covered with the mixture.

3 Marinate the chicken for an hour, turning it occasionally.

4 While the chicken is marinating, **peel** the skin from the garlic, and finely **chop** it.

5 When the chicken has marinated, heat the oil in a **wok** or frying pan over a medium heat. Add the chopped garlic, the chicken, and the marinade, and **stir-fry** for 7 minutes.

Ready to eat: 1 hour 20 minutes (including 1 hour to marinate). Difficulty **.
Serves 2.

6 Add the water chestnuts, bamboo shoots, and the rest of the lemon juice. Stir-fry for 3 minutes more, then serve.

VEGETARIAN VERSION
You could try making a vegetarian version of this dish by replacing the chicken with vegetables such as mushrooms or mangetout.

Honey chicken

Honey or sugar are regularly used in savoury Chinese dishes. Chinese cooks feel that a small amount of sweet flavour helps balance the savoury or salty ingredients in a dish. Try serving this with plain boiled rice (see page 19).

What you need

A small piece of fresh ginger (about 2cm long)

2 boneless chicken breasts

2 tbsp soy sauce

50ml water

2 tbsp honey

1 tbsp vegetable oil

2 spring onions

What you do

1 **Peel** the skin from the ginger, and **grate** or finely **chop** it.

2 Take any skin off the chicken breasts and **slice** them.

3 In a bowl, mix together the soy sauce, water, honey, and ginger.

4 Heat the oil in a **wok** or frying pan over a medium heat. Add the chicken slices.

5 **Fry** the chicken slices for about 5 minutes, turning them occasionally.

6 Carefully pour the soy sauce mixture into the wok.

7 Bring the liquid in the pan to the **boil**, put the lid on, and let it **simmer** for 10 minutes.

8 Cut the tops and bottoms off the spring onions, and finely chop them.

9 Stir the spring onions into the chicken mixture, then serve.

CHINESE SUGAR

Chinese cooks use two main types of sugar: brown slab sugar and rock candy. Brown slab sugar is pressed into hard, flat slabs and sold in fingers about 15cm long. Rock candy is a pale honey colour, and is sold in lumps that look like crystals. You might find some in oriental food shops.

Noodles with minced pork

This dish is called *mayi hshang shu* in Chinese, which means "ants climbing a tree". The minced pork is thought to look like ants climbing a tree when it is added to the noodles!

What you need

125g fine egg noodles (see page 27)

A small piece of fresh ginger (about 2cm long)

1 clove of garlic

250ml water

1 vegetable stock cube

1 tbsp vegetable oil

225g minced pork

1 tbsp soy sauce

2 tsp sugar

2 spring onions

What you do

1 Put the noodles into a large bowl. Pour over enough warm water to cover them, and leave them to soak for 15 minutes.

2 **Peel** the ginger, and **grate** or finely **chop** it.

3 Peel the garlic and finely chop it.

4 Put the water into a saucepan, and bring it to the **boil**. Crumble the stock cube into the water, and stir until it **dissolves**. **Cover** the pan, and put the stock to one side.

5 Heat the oil in a **wok** or frying pan over a medium heat. Add the minced pork, and **stir-fry** for 5 minutes, until the meat starts to go brown.

6 Add the ginger, garlic, soy sauce, sugar, and vegetable stock to the wok.

7 Carefully **drain** the noodles and stir them into the mixture in the wok. Reduce the heat and **simmer** the mixture for about 15 minutes, until most of the liquid has gone.

8 Cut the tops and bottoms off the spring onions, and finely chop them.

9 Spoon the pork and noodle mixture onto plates, and sprinkle the spring onions over the top.

NOODLES

Egg noodles are made in different sizes – fine, medium, and thick. They are sold in packets, telling you what size they are. Fine noodles are best for this dish, as they mix well with the minced pork. They are sometimes called thread noodles.

Vegetable chow mein

This is a very simple noodle and vegetable dish. Medium egg noodles are the best (see page 27).

What you need

75g mushrooms
75g mangetout
25ml water
130g medium egg
    noodles
1 tbsp vegetable oil
75g canned bamboo
    shoots
2½ tbsp soy sauce

What you do

1 **Slice** the mushrooms.

2 Cut the tops and bottoms off the mangetout.

3 Pour the water into a pan and bring it to the **boil**. Add the noodles, and boil them for about 3 minutes, until they are just beginning to go soft.

4 Carefully tip the noodles into a **colander**, and rinse them in cold water.

5 **Drain** the water from the bamboo shoots by emptying them into a sieve or colander.

6 Heat the oil in a **wok** or frying pan. Add the sliced mushrooms, mangetout, and bamboo shoots, and **stir-fry** for 4 minutes.

Ready to eat: 20 minutes. Difficulty **. Serves 2.

 **7** Add the drained noodles and soy sauce, and stir-fry for about 5 minutes, until the noodles are hot, then serve.

NOODLES TO GO
Tasty noodle dishes are served from food stalls all over China. They are called *xiao chi*, which means "small eats", and they are eaten as snacks or quick meals.

Tofu stir-fry

Tofu tastes quite **bland** on its own, so it is usually cooked with other ingredients which add flavour. In this dish, it is **fried** with enough chilli powder to give it flavour, without making the dish too hot and spicy. If you don't like chilli, just leave it out.

What you need

1 onion

A small piece of fresh ginger (about 2cm long)

1 tbsp vegetable oil

100g tofu

1 tsp chilli powder (optional)

Several leaves of pak choi or other greens (see page 31)

1 tbsp soy sauce

What you do

1 **Peel** the skin from the onion, and finely **chop** it.

2 Peel the skin from the ginger, and **grate** or finely chop it.

3 Cut the tofu into cubes about 2cm across.

4 Heat the oil in a **wok** or frying pan over a medium heat. Add the cubed tofu, chopped ginger, and chilli powder (if using), and fry for about 10 minutes, until the tofu is golden brown.

5 Add the chopped onion to the wok, and **stir-fry** for 3 minutes.

6 Cut the pak choi leaves into bite-sized pieces. Add them and the soy sauce to the wok. Stir-fry for 2 minutes, until the pak choi leaves are just beginning to droop, then serve.

PAK CHOI

Pak choi is a type of Chinese cabbage. It is sometimes known as "bok choy". It has long white stems and green leaves. You can usually find pak choi in oriental food shops, and sometimes in supermarkets. If you can't find pak choi, you can replace it with fresh spinach in this dish.

Celery and prawn salad

This salad can be served on its own as or a side dish.

What you need

2 stalks of celery

2 spring onions

A small piece of fresh ginger (about 2cm long)

100g bean sprouts

50g cooked peeled prawns (**thawed** if frozen)

1 tbsp soy sauce

1 tbsp wine vinegar (red or white)

1 tbsp vegetable oil

What you do

1 Carefully **slice** the celery stalks using a sharp knife.

2 Cut the tops and bottoms off the spring onions, and slice them.

3 **Peel** the skin from the ginger, and **grate** or finely **chop** it.

4 Wash the bean sprouts by putting them into a sieve or **colander** and rinsing them with cold water.

5 Put the chopped celery, spring onion, ginger, bean sprouts, and prawns into a salad bowl.

6 Mix together the soy sauce, vinegar, and oil in a small bowl to make a **dressing** for the salad.

7 Pour the dressing over the salad. Mix everything together and serve.

HOW TO USE CHOPSTICKS

Pick up one chopstick, and hold it between your thumb and first two fingers. This chopstick is the one that will move.

Put the second chopstick between your second and third fingers, and behind your thumb. This chopstick stays still. Move the top chopstick up and down with your thumb and first finger so that the tips of the chopsticks meet.

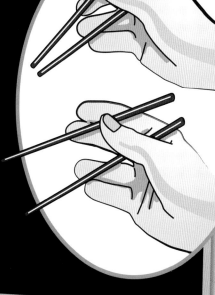

Ginger and spring onion noodles

This noodle dish is an ideal accompaniment for some of the main dishes in this book, such as lemon chicken stir-fry (page 22), honey chicken (page 24), and tofu stir-fry (page 30).

What You need

2 spring onions

small piece fresh ginger (about 2cm long)

130g medium egg noodles

1 tbsp vegetable oil

1 tbsp soy sauce

What You do

1 Cut the tops and bottoms off the spring onions, and finely **chop** them.

2 **Peel** the ginger, and **grate** or finely chop it.

3 Bring a pan of water to the **boil**. Carefully add the noodles, and boil them for about 3 minutes, until they are just beginning to go soft.

4 Tip the noodles into a **colander** to **drain** them, then put them back into the pan. Reduce the heat to low.

5 Add the chopped spring onions, chopped ginger, oil, and soy sauce.

6 Stir everything together and cook for another 2 minutes.

SPRING ONIONS

Spring onions, also known as scallions, are used in many Chinese dishes. They have a milder flavour than ordinary onions, and they cook very quickly. This makes them ideal for stir-fries and other dishes that need to be cooked quickly. The green stems of the spring onions are sometimes shredded or curled into flower shapes to decorate dishes.

Three rice dishes

Here are three different ways of cooking rice to accompany your Chinese meal – coconut rice, rice with peas, and egg fried rice. You could also serve plain boiled rice – see the box on page 19 for how to cook this.

What you need

Coconut rice
Ready to eat:
   25 minutes
140g rice
500ml coconut milk

Rice with peas
Ready to eat:
   25 minutes
140g rice
140g frozen peas
400ml water
1 tbsp soy sauce

Egg fried rice
Ready to eat:
   30 minutes
140g rice
2 tbsp vegetable oil
2 eggs

What you do

Coconut rice

1 Put the rice into a saucepan and add the coconut milk.

2 Bring to the **boil**, then **cover** the pan and **simmer** for 20 minutes, stirring occasionally.

Rice with peas

1 Put the rice and peas into a saucepan and add the water.

2 Bring to the boil, then cover the pan and simmer for 20 minutes, stirring occasionally.

3 Sprinkle the rice with the soy sauce before serving.

Egg fried rice

1 Cook the rice on its own as described in the recipes on page 36.

2 Crack the eggs into a small bowl. **Beat** them with a fork or a whisk until the yolk and the white are mixed.

3 Heat the oil in a **wok** or non-strick frying pan over a medium heat. Add the beaten eggs and **fry** them, stirring all the time, for about 4 minutes.

4 Add the cooked rice to the frying pan, and mix well with the egg.

Egg fried rice

Rice with peas

Coconut rice

Sweet chestnut balls

Chestnuts have been used in Chinese cooking for thousands of years. These sweet chestnut balls are eaten in China as a dessert or a snack.

What you need

200g canned chestnuts

3 tbsp **set** honey

40g icing sugar

1 tsp cinnamon

What you do

1 If the chestnuts are in liquid in the can, **drain** them by pouring the chestnuts into a **colander** or sieve and patting them dry with paper towel.

2 Put the chestnuts and the honey into a food processor or blender. **Blend** together on the highest setting.

3 Put the icing sugar and cinnamon into a bowl, and mix them together with a spoon.

4 Using your fingers, take a little of the chestnut and honey paste out of the food processor or blender. Roll it into a ball.

5 Cover the ball in sugar and cinnamon by rolling it in the mixture in the bowl.

6 Repeat steps 4 and 5 with the rest of the chestnut and honey paste.

7 Serve the sweet chestnut balls straight away, or keep them in the fridge until you are ready to eat them.

ROAST CHESTNUTS

Roast chestnuts are served all over China. In autumn, chestnut sellers set up stalls on the streets of many Chinese cities, where they roast chestnuts over charcoal.

Chocolate lychees

Lychees are a **tropical** fruit. Originally, they came from southern China, but now people grow them in many tropical countries. They have a very sweet taste, and a texture a bit like jelly. If you are using fresh lychees, you will need to **peel** them, so add about 10 minutes to the "Ready to eat" time.

You can melt the chocolate in a heatproof bowl that fits on top of your saucepan or in a microwave oven in a non-metallic, microwave-proof bowl.

What you need

80g plain chocolate
200g canned or fresh lychees

What you do

1 Break the chocolate into pieces and put them into the bowl.

2 If you are using a microwave oven, cook the chocolate on medium power for 1 minute and then stir until melted. Carry on from step 7.

3 If you are using a hob, put 400ml water into the saucepan. Heat the water over a medium heat until it is just bubbling at the edges, but not **boiling**. Reduce the heat to low.

4 Put the bowl of chocolate on top of the pan without letting it touch the hot water. Leave until the chocolate melts (probably about 5 minutes).

Ready to eat: 1 hour 25 minutes (including 1 hour to chill). Difficulty **.
Serves 2.

5 While the chocolate is melting, if you are using canned lychees, **drain** them by pouring them into a sieve or **colander**. Pat them dry with paper towel.

 6 Turn off the heat on the hob. Using oven gloves, take the bowl of melted chocolate from the top of the pan.

7 Pick up a lychee, and dip one half of it into the melted chocolate. Put the lychee onto a sheet of greaseproof paper. (Use a cocktail stick to help pick up the lychee if you need to.)

8 Repeat step 7 with all the lychees.

9 Put the chocolate-coated lychees to **chill** in the fridge for about an hour to let the chocolate harden, then serve.

Orange tea

Chinese people have grown and drunk tea for thousands of years. This recipe suggests using oranges to make a sweet tea that is served at the end of a meal. You could try grapefruit or canned pineapple. Have fun experimenting!

What you need

2 oranges
1 tbsp cornflour
50g sugar
400ml water

What you do

1 **Peel** the oranges, then **chop** them into small pieces.

2 Put the cornflour and sugar into a saucepan and add the water.

3 Put the saucepan over a medium heat, and bring the mixture to the **boil**, stirring all the time.

4 Add the orange pieces.

5 Reduce the heat to medium and **simmer** the tea for another 5 minutes. Serve and drink with care as it will be hot!

DIFFERENT TEAS

Many different types of tea are produced in China. Different areas of the country produce different flavour teas. Some of the Chinese teas you might be able to find in shops and supermarkets include:

- oolong: a smooth, fruity, slightly spicy tea
- lapsang souchong: a strongly flavoured tea, in which the leaves are smoked to give a smoky smell and flavour
- gunpowder: a tea made from greyish tea leaves

Further information

Here are some places to find out more about life in China and Chinese cooking.

Books

Cooking the Chinese Way by Ling Yu (Lerner, 2009)
Food in China by Polly Goodman (PowerKids Press, 2008)
Foods of China by Barbara Sheen (KidHaven Press, 2006)
The Second International Cookbook for Kids by Matthew Locricchio
 (Marshall Cavendish, 2008)
The Young Chef's Chinese Cookbook by Frances Lee (Crabtree, 2007

Websites

www.apples4theteacher.com/holidays/chinese-new-year/recipes

http://chinesefood.about.com/od/resourceschinesecooking/a/
teachingcooking.htm

http://kids-cooking.suite101.com/article.cfm/chinese_food_recipes_
for_kids

www.yumyum.com/rsearch.htm?cat=browse&title=browse&keyword
=Chinese

www.globalgourmet.com/destinations/china

Healthy eating

This diagram shows the types and proportion of food you should eat to stay healthy. Eat plenty of foods from the *bread, rice, potatoes, pasta* group and plenty from the *fruit and vegetables* group. Eat some foods from the *milk and dairy* group and the *meat, fish, eggs, beans* group. Foods from the smallest group are not necessary for a healthy diet so eat these in small amounts or only occasionally.

Many Chinese dishes are served with rice or noodles, which belong to the bread, rice, potatoes, pasta group. In China, people eat some meat and fish, as well as tofu, which is made from soya beans. They also use lots of fresh vegetables, so you can see how healthy Chinese cooking is!

↑ The Eatwell food plate shows the proportion of food from each food group you should eat to achieve a healthy, balanced diet. This takes account of everything you eat, including snacks.

Glossary

beat mix something together strongly using a fork, spoon, or whisk

bland without much flavour

blend mix ingredients together in a blender or food processor

boil cook a liquid on the hob. Boiling liquid bubbles and steams strongly.

chill put something in the fridge to make it cold before serving it

chop cut something into pieces using a knife

colander bowl-shaped container with holes in it, used for draining vegetables and straining

cover put a lid on a pan, or foil over a dish

defrost allow something that is frozen to thaw

dissolve mix something until it disappears into a liquid

drain remove liquid, usually by pouring something into a colander or sieve

dressing oil and vinegar sauce for a salad

fry cook something in oil in a pan

grate break something, such as cheese, into small pieces using a grater

grill cook something under the grill

marinate soak something, such as meat or fish, in a mixture called a marinade before cooking, so that it absorbs the taste of the mixture

peel remove the skin of a fruit or vegetable

protein a body-building material found in some foods, such as beans, eggs, and meat

set food, such as jelly or eggs, that is not liquid any more is called set

simmer cook a liquid on the hob. Simmering liquid bubbles and steams gently.

slice cut something into thin, flat pieces

stir-fry fry something very quickly in a wok or frying pan, stirring all the time

thaw defrost something which has been frozen

tropical a hot, wet climate

vegetarian food that does not contain meat or fish. People who don't eat meat or fish are called vegetarians.

wok a round, deep pan used for cooking many Chinese dishes

Index

accompaniments
  boiled rice 19
  celery and prawn salad 32
  coconut rice 36
  egg fried rice 37
  ginger and spring onion
      noodles 34
  rice with peas 36
bamboo shoots
  lemon chicken stir-fry 22
  mushroom and water
      chestnut soup 12
  vegetable chow mein 28
bean sprouts
  celery and prawn salad 32
  boiled rice 19
  celery and prawn salad 32
  Chinese fish cakes 18
  chocolate lychees 40
  coconut rice 36
desserts
  chocolate lychees 40
  sweet chestnut balls 38
drinks
  orange tea 42
egg fried rice 37
ginger 8
  ginger and spring onion
      noodles 34
  honey chicken 24
  noodles with minced pork 26
  prawns with ginger sauce 16
  stir-fried fish with mushrooms
      and cucumber 18
ginger and spring onion noodles 34
honey chicken 24
lemon chicken stir-fry 22
main courses
  Chinese fish cakes 18
  honey chicken 24
  lemon chicken stir-fry 22

noodles with minced pork 26
stir-fried fish with mushrooms
    and cucumber 20
tofu stir-fry 30
vegetable chow mein 28
mushrooms
  mushroom and water
      chestnut soup 12
  stir-fried fish with mushrooms
      and cucumber 20
  vegetable chow mein 28
mushroom and water chestnut soup 12
noodles 9
  ginger and spring onion noodles 34
  noodles with minced pork 26
  vegetable chow mein 28
noodles with minced pork 26
orange tea 42
prawns with ginger sauce 16
rice 9
  boiled rice 19
  coconut rice 36
  egg fried rice 37
  rice with peas 36
starters and snacks
  chocolate lychees 40
  mushroom and water
      chestnut soup 12
  prawns with ginger sauce 16
  sweet chestnut balls 38
  stir-fried fish with mushrooms
      and cucumber 20
sweet chestnut balls 38
tea 43
  orange tea 42
tofu 9
  tofu stir-fry 30
vegetable chow mein 28
water chestnuts
  lemon chicken stir-fry 22
  mushroom and water
      chestnut soup 12